PICTURES
of the gone world

LAWRENCE FERLINGHETTI

ENLARGED EDITION, 1995

CITY LIGHTS BOOKS
San Francisco

CITY LIGHTS BOOKS are edited by Lawrence Ferlinghetti
and Nancy J. Peters and published at the City Lights
Bookstore, 261 Columbus Avenue, San Francisco,
CA 94133.

Contents

1   Away above a harborful
2   Just as I used to say
3   In hintertime Praxiteles
4   In Paris in a loud dark winter
5   Not too long
6   And the Arabs asked terrible questions
7   Yes
8   Sarolla's women in their picture hats
9   'Truth is not the secret of a few'
10   for all I know maybe she was happier
11   Fortune
12   And she 'like a young year
13   It was a face which darkness could kill
14   So
15   funny fantasies are never so real as oldstyle romances
16   Three maidens went over the land
17   Terrible
18   London
19   with bells for hooves in sounding streets
20   That fellow on the boattrain who insisted
21   Heaven
22   crazy
23   Dada would have liked a day like this
24   Picasso's acrobats epitomize the world
25   The world is a beautiful place
26   Reading Yeats I do not think
27   sweet and various the woodlark
28   And each poem a picture
29   Bicyclists among the trees by the lake
30   A hole in a redwood tree
31   Ah there's the moon

32 'Pale horse pale rider'
33 Three Wapiti elk in heartland America
34 Surfers are poets too
35 Her voice was full of Yes
36 People kept coming in and looking
37 At the Hopper house
38 Loneliness
39 A blockage in the bowel
40 On upper Fifth Avenue
41 In an old black & white photo
42 She looked so good in the morning
43 Why don't you sometime try —
44 As in a play by Jean-Paul Sartre
45 The classical masks

1

Away above a harborful
                           of caulkless houses
among the charley noble chimneypots
                           of a rooftop rigged with clotheslines
        a woman pastes up sails
                           upon the wind
    hanging out her morning sheets
                           with wooden pins
            O lovely mammal
                           her nearly naked breasts
                throw taut shadows
                           when she stretches up
    to hang at last the last of her
                           so white washed sins
        but it is wetly amorous
                           and winds itself about her
            clinging to her skin
                           So caught with arms upraised
    she tosses back her head
                           in voiceless laughter
and in choiceless gesture then
                           shakes out gold hair

while in the reachless seascape spaces

                    between the blown white shrouds

    stand out the bright steamers

                           to kingdom come

2

Just as I used to say
          love comes harder to the aged
because they've been running
          on the same old rails too long
  and then when the sly switch comes along
          they miss the turn
  and burn up the wrong rail while
          the gay caboose goes flying
  and the steamengine driver don't recognize
          them new electric horns
and the aged run out on the rusty spur
          which ends up in
     the dead grass where
  the rusty tincans and bedsprings and old razor
      blades and moldy mattresses
          lie
  and the rail breaks off dead
          right there
  though the ties go on awhile
          and the aged
  say to themselves
    Well
      this must be the place
    we were supposed to lie down

And they do

        while the bright saloon careens along away
on a high
      hilltop
        its windows full of bluesky and lovers
   with flowers
         their long hair streaming
           and all of them laughing
    and waving and
          whispering to each other
  and looking out and
         wondering what that graveyard
   where the rails end
        is

In hintertime Praxiteles
                    laid about him with a golden maul
        striking into stone
                        his alabaster ideals
uttering all
            the sculptor's lexicon
                            in visible syllables
        He cast bronze trees
                        petrified a chameleon on one
        made stone doves
                    fly
                        His calipers measured bridges
            and lovers
                and certain other superhumans whom
he caught upon their dusty way
                            to death

        They never reached it then

                        You still can almost see
                their breath
                        Their stone eyes staring
    thru three thousand years
                    allay our fears of aging

        although Praxiteles himself
                        at twenty-eight lay dead

                for sculpture isn't for
                                    young men
        as Constantin Brancusi
                                at a later hour
                        said

4

In Paris in a loud dark winter

        when the sun was something in Provence

when I came upon the poetry

        of René Char

    I saw Vaucluse again

        in a summer of sauterelles

  its fountains full of petals

        and its river thrown down

  through all the burnt places

        of that almond world

and the fields full of silence

        though the crickets sang

  with their legs

        And in the poet's plangent dream I saw

no Lorelei upon the Rhone

        nor angels debarked at Marseilles

but couples going nude into the sad water

        in the profound lasciviousness of spring

in an algebra of lyricism

        which I am still deciphering

Not too long

        after the beginning of time

upon a nine o'clock

        of a not too hot

           summer night

  standing in the door

        of the NEW PISA

           under the forgotten

      plaster head of DANTE

          waiting for a table

     and watching

        Everything

     was a man with a mirror for a head

which didn't look so abnormal at that

          except that

    real ears stuck out

         and he had a sign

     which read

A POEM IS A MIRROR WALKING DOWN A STRANGE STREET

       but anyway

   as I was saying

      not too long after the beginning

  of time

                              this man who was all eyes

            had no mouth
                              All he could do was show people
what he meant
                  And it turned out
                                          he claimed to be
                  a painter

                              But anyway
            this painter
                        who couldn't talk or tell anything
                        about what he
                                          meant
            looked like just about the happiest painter
                  in all the world
standing there
                  taking it all 'in'
                                    and reflecting
            Everything
                        in his great big

                                    Hungry Eye

                  but anyway

      so it was I saw reflected there

                              Four walls covered with pictures
of the leaning tower of Pisa
                  all of them leaning in different directions

Five booths with tables

Fifteen tables without booths

One bar
            with one bartender looking like a
                              baseball champ
            with a lot of naborhood trophies
                    hung up behind

Three waitresses of various sizes and faces
                    one as big as a little fox terrier
                    one as large as a small sperm whale
                    one as strange as an angei
            but all three
                    with the same eyes
One kitchendoor with one brother cook
                                    standing in it
                    with the same eyes

                                    and about
one hundredandsixtythree people all talking and
waving and laughing and eating and drinking and
smiling and frowning and shaking heads and opening
mouths and putting forks and spoons in them and
chewing and swallowing all kinds of produce and
sitting back and relaxing maybe and drinking coffee
and lighting cigarettes and getting up and so on
                                    and so off

                         into the night
without ever noticing
                    the man with the mirrorhead
       below the forgotten
                    plasterhead of DANTE
                              looking down
                    at everyone
                              with the same eyes
       as if he were still searching
                              Everywhere
              for his lost Beatrice
                         but with just a touch
              of devilish lipstick
                              on the very tip
              of his nose

And the Arabs asked terrible questions
and the Pope didn't know what to say and the people
ran around in wooden shoes asking which way was the
head of Midas facing and everyone said

No instead of Yes

While still forever in the Luxembourg
gardens in the fountains of the Medici were the
fat red goldfish and the fat white goldfish
and the children running around the pool
pointing and piping
Des poissons rouges!
Des poissons rouges!

but they ran off
and a leaf unhooked itself
and fell upon the pool
and lay like an eye winking
circles

and then the pool was very

                              still
                              and there was a dog
                    just standing there
                              at the edge of the pool
                         looking down
                              at the tranced fish
          and not barking
                         or waving its funny tail or
                                        anything

               so that

                    for a moment then

          in the late November dusk

     silence hung like a lost idea
                              and a statue turned

                    its head

7

Yes
           and we stood about
                       up in Central Park
     dropping coins in the fountains
                       and a harlequin
           came naked among
                       the nursemaids
and caught them picking their noses
                 when they should have been

     dancing

8

Sarolla's women in their picture hats
stretched upon his canvas beaches
beguiled the Spanish
Impressionists

And were they fraudulent
pictures
of the world
the way the light played on them
creating illusions
of love?

I cannot help but think
that their 'reality'
was almost as real as
my memory of today

when the last sun hung on the hills
and I heard the day falling
like the gulls that fell
almost to land

while the last picnickers lay
and loved in the blowing yellow broom
resisted and resisting
tearing themselves apart
again

again

until the last hot hung climax
which could at last no longer be resisted
made them moan

And night's trees stood up

'Truth is not the secret of a few'
                              yet
you would maybe think so
                    the way some
          librarians
and cultural ambassadors and
                    especially museum directors
                                        act

     you'd think they had a corner
                              on it
          the way they
                    walk around shaking
their high heads and
                    looking as if they never
     went to the bath
          room or anything

     But I wouldn't blame them
if I were you
          They say the Spiritual is best conceived
in abstract terms
               and then too
     walking around in museums always makes me
     want to
               'sit down'
     I always feel so
                    constipated
     in those
               high altitudes

for all I know maybe she was happier

                          than anyone

that lone crone in the shawl

                on the orangecrate train

    with the little tame bird

              in her handkerchief

        crooning

           to it all the time

                    mia mascotta

  mia mascotta

        and none of the sunday excursionists

        with their bottles and their baskets

        paying any

              attention

   and the coach

        creaking on through cornfields

  so slowly that

        butterflies

        blew in and out

Fortune

has its cookies to give out

which is a good thing

since it's been a long time since

that summer in Brooklyn
when they closed off the street
one hot day
and the

FIREMEN

turned on their hoses

and all the kids ran out in it

in the middle of the street

and there were

maybe a couple dozen of us

out there

with the water squirting up

to the

sky

and all over

us

there was maybe only six of us

                                     kids altogether

        running around in our

                              barefeet and birthday

     suits

        and I remember Molly but then

the firemen stopped squirting their hoses

        all of a sudden and went

                back in

                their firehouse

                and

        started playing pinochle again

              just as if nothing

                 had ever

                           happened

while I remember Molly

                      looked at me and

     ran in

because I guess really we were the only ones there

And she 'like a young year
                        walking thru the earth'
in the Bois de Boulogne that time
                        or as I remember her
        stepping out of a bathtub
                        in that gold flat she had
                    corner of
                        Boulevard des Italiens

        Oh they say she tried everything
                            before the end
took up television and crosswords
                            even crocheting
        and things like that
                        and came to have the air
            before the end
                    (as her favorite poet described her)
of 'always carrying flowers
                    toward some far
                            abandoned tomb'

which doesn't surprise me now
                        that I come to think of it

        The struck seed was in her

It was a face which darkness could kill
                              in an instant
   a face as easily hurt
                 by laughter or light

   'We *think* differently at night'
                           she told me once
lying back languidly

                     And she would quote Cocteau

'I feel there is an angel in me' she'd say
                     'whom I am constantly shocking'

   Then she would smile and look away
            light a cigarette for me
                                 sigh and rise
and stretch
          her sweet anatomy

                        let fall a stocking

14

So

    he sed

        You think yer pretty snappy

don't you now

      with your sunnyside layer up

    and your bloomin big tits like flowers

    and your way of always looking so inno

             cent

   holding a flower between your teeth and

        laughing with your

  eyes

    Well

     maybe we cud go somewheres

        (he sed)

   after th'show

funny fantasies are never so real as oldstyle romances
    where the hero has a heroine who has
        long black braids and lets
                nobody
  kiss her ever
        and everybody's trying all the time to
run away with her
      and the hero is always drawing his
  (sic) sword and
      tilting at ginmills and
             forever telling her he
loves her and has only honorable intentions and
honorable mentions
       and no one ever beats him at
            anything
but then finally one day
      she who has always been so timid
offs with her glove and says
       (though not in so many big words)
Let's lie down somewheres

          baby

Three maidens went over the land
One carried a piece of bread
                              in the hand
One said
              Let's divide it and cut it

And they strolled thru a red forest
and in the red forest
                              there stood a red church
and in the red church
                        stood a red altar
and upon the red altar
                          lay a red knife
and now we come to the parable
                                  They
took the red knife and wounded
                              their bread
and where they cut with the
                          so red knife

                                it was red

17

Terrible

     a horse at night

standing hitched alone

       in the still street

and whinnying

       as if some sad nude astride him

had gripped hot legs on him

     and sung

       a sweet high hungry

single syllable

London

crossfigured
creeping with trams

and the artists on sundays
in the summer
all 'tracking Nature'
in the suburbs

It
could have been anyplace
but it wasn't
It was
London

and when someone shouted over

that they had got a model

I ran out across the court

but then
when the model started taking off
her clothes
there was nothing underneath
I mean to say
she took off her shoes
and found no feet
took off her top
and found no tit
under it

and I must say she did look

a bit

ASTOUNDED

just standing there
looking down
at where her legs were

not

But so very carefully then

she put her clothes back on
and as soon as she was dressed again

completely

she was completely

all right

Do it again! cried someone

rushing for his easel

But she was afraid to

and gave up modelling

and forever after

slept in her clothes

with bells for hooves in sounding streets

that terrible horse the unicorn

came on

and cropped a medlar from a tree
                              and where he dropped the seed
        sprang up a virgin

                    oh she sprang up upon his back
    and rode off tittering to a stair
                        where pieces of string lay scattered
        everywhere

            Now when she saw the string so white
so lovely and so beautiful
                    and looking like
                              Innocence itself
    she got down and reached for a nice
                              straight piece

            but it had a head
            and it bit
                    her beautiful place

                              So (she said)

        this is how it all began

                        Next time I'll know

    But it was too late and they buried her

That fellow on the boattrain who insisted
              on playing blackjack
              had teeth that stuck out
        like lighthouses on a rocky coast

but
  he had no eyes to see
                              the dusk flash past

        horses in orchards
                              noiselessly running
bunches of birds
              thrown up

        and the butterflies of yesterday
              that flittered on
                 my mind

Heaven

        was only half as far that night

at the poetry recital

        listening to the burnt phrases

when I heard the poet have

        a rhyming erection

then look away with a

        lost look

'Every animal' be said at last

'After intercourse is sad'

But the back-row lovers
        looked oblivious

    and glad

crazy

      to be alive in such a strange

             world

with the band playing schmaltz

            in the classic bandshell

              and the people

    on the benches under the clipped trees

             and girls

  on the grass

        and the breeze blowing and the streamers

   streaming

    and a fat man with a graflex

    and a dark woman with a dark dog she called

               Lucia

    and a cat on a leash

    and a pekinese with a blond baby

    and a cuban in a fedora

    and a bunch of boys posing for a group

             picture

and just then

    while the band went right on playing

             schmaltz

a midget ran past shouting and waving his hat

            at someone

    and a young man with a gay campaignbutton

came up and said

        Are you by any chance a registered

            DEMOCRAT?

Dada would have liked a day like this
                              with its various very realistic
                unrealities
                         each about to become
        too real for its locality
                         which is never quite remote enough
            to be Bohemia

Dada would have loved a day like this
                                with its light-bulb sun
          which shines so differently
                              for different people
          but which still shines the same
                                   on everyone
                         and on everything
                                      such as

          a bird on a bench about to sing

                         a plane in a gilded cloud

a dishpan hand
              waving at a window

                              or a phone about to ring

            or a mouth about to give up
                                smoking

or a new newspaper
with its new news story
of a cancerous dancer

Yes Dada would have died for a day like this
with its sweet street carnival
and its too real funeral
just passing thru it
with its real dead dancer
so beautiful and dumb
in her shroud
and her last lover lost
in the unlonely crowd
and its dancer's darling baby
about to say Dada
and its passing priest
about to pray
Dada
and offer his so transcendental
apologies

Yes Dada would have loved a day like this
with its not so accidental
analogies

Picasso's acrobats epitomize the world

and there were eighty churches in Paris
which I
had never entered
and my hotel's door
smiled terribly

and words were trombones
incoherent parrots
chattering idols

but that night I dreamt of Picasso
opening doors and closing exits
opening doors and closing exits in the world

I dreamt
he painted a Picasso
in my room
shouting all the time
Pas symbolique!
C'est pas
symbolique!

CITY LIGHTS BOOKS

Open Everyday 10AM to Midnight
A Literary Meetingplace since 1953

1068262 Reg 1 2:37 pm 07/09/15

S PICTURES OF THE G   1 @   7.95   7.95
SUBTOTAL   7.95
SALES TAX - 8.75%   .70

The world is a beautiful place
                              to be born into
if you don't mind happiness
                    not always being
                              so very much fun
    if you don't mind a touch of hell
                              now and then
        just when everything is fine
                              because even in heaven
            they don't sing
                              all the time

    The world is a beautiful place
                                  to be born into
    if you don't mind some people dying
                              all the time

            or maybe only starving
                              some of the time
        which isn't half so bad
                              if it isn't you

Oh the world is a beautiful place
                              to be born into
        if you don't much mind
                        a few dead minds
            in the higher places
                              or a bomb or two
            now and then
                        in your upturned faces
or such other improprieties
                              as our Name Brand society
                  is prey to
                        with its men of distinction
        and its men of extinction
                              and its priests
            and other patrolmen

                              and its various segregations
and congressional investigations
                              and other constipations
            that our fool flesh
                        is heir to

Yes the world is the best place of all
                              for a lot of such things as
          making the fun scene
                    and making the love scene
and making the sad scene
          and singing low songs and having inspirations
     and walking around
                    looking at everything
                              and smelling flowers
     and goosing statues
                    and even thinking
                              and kissing people and
          making babies and wearing pants
                              and waving hats and
          dancing
                    and going swimming in rivers
          on picnics
               in the middle of the summer
     and just generally
                    'living it up'

Yes
     but then right in the middle of it
                         comes the smiling

                    mortician

Reading Yeats I do not think
                          of Ireland
but of midsummer New York
                       and of myself back then
      reading that copy I found
                     on the Thirdavenue El

     the El
         with its flyhung fans
   and its signs reading
            SPITTING IS FORBIDDEN

     the El
         careening thru its thirdstory world
with its thirdstory people
             in their thirdstory doors
looking as if they had never heard
                of the ground

     an old dame
           watering her plant
or a joker in a straw

                    putting a stickpin in his peppermint tie
and looking just like he had nowhere to go
                                        but coneyisland

            or an undershirted guy
                                rocking in his rocker
watching the El pass by
                as if he expected it to be different
        each time

            Reading Yeats I do not think
                            of Arcady
and of its woods which Yeats thought dead
                                I think instead
            of all the gone faces
                    getting off at midtown places
        with their hats and their jobs
        and of that lost book I had
                    with its blue cover and its white inside
where a pencilhand had written
                HORSEMAN, PASS BY!

sweet and various the woodlark

    who sings at the unbought gate

and yet how many

    wild beasts

        how many mad

  in the civil thickets

      Hölderlin

        in his stone tower

or in that kind carpenter's house

      at Tübingen

    or then Rimbaud

      his 'nightmare and logic'

  a sophism of madness

But we have our own more recent

      who also fatally assumed

that some direct connection

      does exist between

  language and reality

      word and world

    which is a laugh

      if you ask me

I too have drunk and seen

      the spider

And each poem a picture
                    at an exhibition
            upon a blank wall
                        made of concrete chaos
                Colors
                        caught in chaos
            Sounds compounded
                        of chaos
    Meaning
            made of chaos
                        'gathered from the air'

    And every poem 'a raid on the inarticulate'

And all about to fall
                poet and poem and wall and all
        back into it

Bicyclists among the trees by the lake

Piano music slow in the distance

The summer air is heavy
                              with   desiring
The future lover
                    winds through the woods
        trailing   her   purple scarf
                              toward her future lover
                    or a girl in a long white dress
                              and a picture hat
                        strolls across the lawn to Gatsby
It's all an unfinished film
                    for which there is no *finis*
                              (so we would like to think)
                    seen through a telefoto lens
                in which the future couple
                    will have future children
                    in real time
                    who will run through the woods
                              each to his or her own future
And they reproduce themselves
                    and they are multiplied
                              a trillion trillion trillion times
And the film-loop runs on
                    and on and on and on
                              with many a re-take
And as through the wrong end

of a telescope

we see the myriad antic figures

forever disappearing

over the far horizon

As if the quivering meat-wheel tape

(we would like to think)

could never break

A hole in a redwood tree

through which we see

the warp of

time & history

As through three thousand rings

the light sings

Ah there's the moon
        circling the earth
          like a halo a head
      a cynosure of celestial forces

Ah yes the moon at night
           indeed might somehow be
     on such a flight
        reflecting as it does the light
           of Great God Sun

And we down here
     blind in our courses
        still denying it
           when day is done

'Pale horse pale rider'

And the man on the horse
                          is Death
    Across the lone prairies
                          to Tombstone
    where at the Bird Cage Theater
                they are whooping it up
A deal with the Devil and
                          a soul is for sale

And so begins another tale in which
            out here on the left side of the world
            still anything can happen

And does

Three Wapiti elk in heartland America
     with full spread of antlers
   Racks like bare trees
        hung in the sky
out in a meadowmarsh
    in hot dry sunlight
      above the tree line
        in Rocky Mountain Park
  the three of them
      silent and still
        and watching everything
  guarding the entrance to
       their kingdom
And further on up
    at twelve thousand feet
only the heads and horns of
     a whole herd of elk
   visible over a ridge
    the heads all turned to us
       transfixed with the sight of us
      curious bipeds
        hung with cameras
   interlopers loping along
    on our hind legs
      with baseball caps and
        plastic tote-bags

And the benevolent and protective
                                    order of the elk
                    watching all
                                    with the trepidation of
                                                    palace guards
                    knowing they are
                                    fatally outnumbered

Surfers are poets too
>>> if you look at it that way
>>> at least in the western part of the West
They too are looking
>> for the perfect wave
>>> with the perfect rhythm sublime
They too are looking for the endless light
>>> at the end of the tube of time
They too would fly
>> through an eye of an needle
They too are realists
>> and know a killer-wave when they see one
These are not cyberpunks
>> surfing through cyberspace
They are sailors who know
>>> that the sea like life has its rages
>>> and can be a merciless monster
>>> when it wants to
> dashing the poem of your endless summer
>>> on the rimeless rocks of outrageous fortune

Her voice was full of Yes
     but her ego said No
  (it was much too big
    like a sailingship with
      too much keel
        never able to heel over)
And the contradiction more
     than any skipper
       could handle
Except for one sly old
   fly fisherman
    who thought he knew
     how to bait her
       with a light rod
    so that she'd
     make a run for it
        and bite
And he hooked her good all right
    But sank straight down with her
        to God

People kept coming in and looking
> at the half-alive fish on ice
>> which they could choose
>>> to have cooked for them

Only many turned away and
> went right out of the restaurant
> as if displeased
> by the awfully strange look
> the fish gave them
> or with the general expression of the fish
> and with the awful gestures he made
> (if you call gasping for breath a gesture)

And they not wanting really
to be that much involved
in the half-life
of a fish

At the Hopper house
                on the beach at Truro
I look back up at it
                on its high bluff
And I am Edward Hopper
                famous American painter
      sprawled on the hillside
                on the beach grasses
      looking back up at
                Hopper's World
      where he lived all those
                windblown years
hardly as lonely as
      the people in his paintings
      in their all-night diners
                Sunday morning storefronts
      bare-bulb bedrooms
                lighthouses in sun
      summer evening porches
      houses by the railrooad
                Victorian facades
                    of emptiness

And yet would I paint them differently now
                          at the tail end of our twisted century
          as if overpopulation now
                          had really overcome
                              our enormous solitudes
                              in which a symbol of success is still
                              an isolated house
                                  on a hill

Loneliness
              is not as wildly exhilarating
      as Rimbaudian insanity
              (with bawds in Belgium
                    or boys in Brooklyn)
    and not as far-out as
        chilling yourself with
            various forms of
                fancy inhalations
        or other willful
                skillful excitations
                    of the senses
But it too kills the unwary
    who buy flowers from itinerant arabs
              on café terraces
      for nudes passing by
                in second floor windows
      who may or may not
            be gay or anyway
      won't even glance down
                    at the clown
            waving the flowers

A blockage in the bowel
 causes hang-ups in dreams
  or so it sometimes seems
as for instance when
 Sisyphus keeps trying all the time
  to roll that boulder up
  and it comes always rolling back
   down upon him
 or as when we cannot get across
   that symbolic railroad crossing
  where the train keeps bearing down on us
   all the time
  where you sit helpless at the helm
  of a wheelless
   Presidential limousine
  with fifty-one clowns in the back
  all wearing nothing but
   Stars & Stripes
  and all of them singing
   God Help America!

On upper Fifth Avenue
                    by Grand Army Plaza

   the dignified doorman
                    with the scrambled eggs
                                on his visor

   (looking like General MacArthur
                    about to wade ashore)

Opens the door

In an old black & white photo
    a made-up angel
        in a highschool parade
with 'a mixture of innocence and eye-shadow'
    (the caption tells us)
       'and those uncertain wings . . .'
The uncertainty being whether
      this nymph errant
        would ever be able to
       fly through
          the uncertain weather of
    her adolescence

And I am smitten
      (by the lovebug bitten)
  as she passes on her float
     moving her wings
        ever so slightly
   Her eyes on Remote

She looked so good in the morning
I thought she'd had her face fixed overnight
And I murmured I'll look at you
                         instead of the dawn outside
And she
      and she
            opened her eyes so very slightly
                  that I fell into those
                        unfathomable
              deep blue depths
            through which what might have been
                  the true mute image of herself
                          very gravely looked out

Why don't you sometime try —

       cried the poet to the painter

  (totally turned off
        by the silence of painting)

Why don't you sometime try
      and see what you can do
          to break out of it

    Just try to show
        with your dumb brush
   Just try to show
       with your mute eye
    How the earth trembles
       as lovers after loving
          echo like bells

As in a play by Jean-Paul Sartre
       in which the past repeats itself
And the dice
      have already
           been thrown
The hero swims in circles
         returning & returning
And arrives at the same
           whirlpools
         and the same conclusions
   by different paths each time
Arrives at the same final choices
    by totally different arguments
      but always dictated by the same still voice
              within himself
(the road not taken always the same)

So that the same mistakes are made
            over & over
  as if by a surgeon
      whose original incisions
        were fatal from the beginning
Or the aviator
     flying routes not flown before
          not shown on any map
     falls by the same flaws
         to the same earth
     falls by the same laws
         into the same lap

Yet on the other hand
    the hero with the fatal flaws
        may find they are very much
                            to his liking
                and guide him lightly
                    at his own pace
                as he sets forth upon his biking
                    to re-articulate in his own lingo
                        'the uncreated conscience' of
                                his far-out time and place

The classical masks of

           tragedy and comedy

    superimposed

        upon each other

      through which the poet speaks

                simultaneously

    make his weeping voice

        sometimes burst out

            rapsodically

  in riotous

        uncontrollable laughter

So that naturally

    the most Absurd

        true-life tragicomedies

            follow after